In Passionate Pursuit: Capturing the American Women's Movement in Art
Photographs by Dr. Alessandra Comini, University Distinguished Professor
of Art History Emerita, Southern Methodist University

Mary H. Dana Women Artists Series,
Mabel Smith Douglass Library Galleries
Rutgers, The State University of New Jersey

September 12 - October 15, 2006

curators
Judith K. Brodsky
Ferris Olin

text by
Judith K. Brodsky

The Mary H. Dana Women Artists Series at the Mabel Smith Douglass Library is celebrating its 35th year. The longest running venue for exhibiting the work of women artists, the series was the idea of Joan Snyder who studied art at Douglass and realized that while the student body consisted of women, the entire visual arts faculty was male. Since 1971, the Series has shown more than 400 artists, some well known and some emerging. Over the ensuing four decades the Dana Women Artist Series has received national recognition as an alternate space that supports women artists' aesthetic and intellectual contributions to the visual arts, and it remains a mainstay of the Feminist Art Movement.

It is only fitting that as the inaugural exhibition celebrating the Series' 35th year, we show Alessandra Comini's candid photographs of women active in creating and sustaining the Feminist Art Movement. Dr. Comini, distinguished professor emerita, at Southern Methodist University has been photographing these women since the early 1970s. Many of the individuals pictured were also working as agents of change to bring the voices of women artists and women art professionals to the fore, as well as the impact of women in politics and the public sphere, among them Bella Abzug and Gloria Steinem.

This exhibition also falls under the umbrella of The Feminist Art Project (TFAP). Dr. Ferris Olin and Professor Judith K. Brodsky are facilitating TFAP at Rutgers with a national committee that includes the artists Judy Chicago, Susan Fisher Sterling, deputy director of the National Museum of Women in the Arts, Maura Reilly, curator, Elizabeth A. Sackler Center for Feminist Art, Brooklyn Museum, Dena Muller, immediate past president, Women's Caucus for Art, and Leslie King Hammond, dean, Graduate Studies, Maryland Institute College of Art. The late Arlene Raven was also a member of the national committee. Many exhibitions and other events will be held over the next few years nationally, as part of TFAP. Rutgers also houses the Women Artists Archive National Directory, Institute for Women and Art, and the Miriam Schapiro Archive for the papers of women artists.

Here is Muriel Magenta caught photographing Alessandra Comini, as Comini, herself is photographing Magenta. Comini, distinguished professor emerita, at Southern Methodist University has been photographing the women pictured in this exhibition and publication since the early 1970s. She and her partner, the late Eleanor Tufts, also a professor in art history at Southern Methodist, were among the founders of the Women's Caucus for Art in 1972 when women art professionals who belonged to the College Art Association became aware of discrimination both in the CAA and in the field.

This is the first time that this historical archive documenting the faces of the women involved in the Feminist Art Movement has been exhibited. The photos included in the exhibition are only a small sampling. Hundreds more remain in Comini's archive.

We want to thank Alessandra Comini for sharing her photographs with us. As curators, we also wish to express our appreciation to Sara Harrington, director of the Mary H. Dana Women Artists Series for giving us the opportunity to mount this exhibition. We want to thank Joe Nanashe for transforming Dr. Comini's slides into exhibition format and Dot Paolo at Rabbet Gallery for framing the work. Our appreciation goes as well to the co-sponsors of the exhibition and accompanying symposium: the Associate Alumnae of Douglass College; Brodsky Center, Mason Gross School of the Arts; Institute for Women and Art; Margery Somers Foster Center, Rutgers University Libraries; Visiting Artists Series, Visual Arts Department, Mason Gross School of the Arts; all at Rutgers, The State University of New Jersey, New Brunswick.

Judith K. Brodsky and Ferris Olin, curators

Alessandra Comini is shown here on the right with Linda Nochlin in the middle and Ann Sutherland Harris on the left.

Nochlin and Harris were the curators of the ground breaking exhibition, *Women Artists 1550 - 1950*, which opened at the Los Angeles County Museum in 1976. This exhibition opened people's eyes to the fact that there had been well known women artists in all periods of art history since the Renaissance. The curators explored the basements of museums in Europe and America where most of the work by women artists was stored. The contrast with today is striking. Now, paintings by artists such as Artemisia Gentileschi, whose name and work were virtually unknown before *Women Artists 1550 - 1950*, hang in the permanent galleries of many museums both in the United States and other countries.

The catalogue of *Women Artists 1550 - 1950* was used as a text book for new classes devoted to the history of women artists which were established at many institutions. The exhibition was also seen at the Brooklyn Museum.

This exhibition revealed how women artists were written out of history. For instance, Angelica Kaufmann was so well known in her time that her funeral procession wound through the streets of Rome where she died. The only other artist in Italian history who received that tribute was Raphael. Until *Women Artists 1550 - 1950*, Angelica Kaufmann was relegated to only a mention in the art history survey books.

Alison Hilton, on the right, is Wright Family Distinguished Chair of Art History and chair of the Art Department at Georgetown University. She is an art historian who specializes in Russian and Soviet art. Recent publications include *Russian Folk Art* and articles on nonconformist art and on women and gender issues in Soviet art; she is currently working on Russian Impressionism.

Dorothy Gillespie is a sculptor and painter, well known for her ribbon-like, pastel-colored metal strips that weave in and out of space creating intricate decorative designs in three dimensions. Long associated with Radford University in Virginia where she holds a special chair, Gillespie was a pioneer in the incubating Feminist Art Movement in New York. She established and ran The Women's Interart Center in New York for many years in the late '60s and during the 1970s. The Women's Interart Center provided one of the earliest alternative venues for women artists from the New York area. Gillespie showed in the Dana Women Artists Series in 1984 - 1985 and 1996.

Miriam Schapiro is one of the founders of the Feminist Art Movement. A well known abstract artist in the 1960s, working with hard edge minimal shapes, Schapiro transformed her own art in the early 1970s to create a style that she felt came from women's experience. This photograph shows Linda Nochlin, on the right, the late Eleanor Tufts in the middle, and Alessandra Comini on the right. in front of one of Schapiro's large fan-shaped paintings.

Schapiro decided that the conventional rectangular canvas had to go--it was identified with male artists who had used it throughout European and American art history. Instead, Schapiro used shapes associated with women and the decorative arts.--the fan, a house shape, a heart, and a kimono. Schapiro wanted to remain a painter. She wanted to infuse painting with a woman's sensibility rather than to give up painting. In addition to using canvas shapes that derive from female lives, she also began to incorporate fabrics, laces, and trims into her work as can be seen here.

Schapiro has a close connection to Rutgers. She served a few years ago as the Lebowitz Lecturer at Douglass College, exhibited in the Dana Women Artists Series several times, most recently in 2005-2005 as the Lebowitz Visiting Artist in Residence, and has created prints at the Brodsky Center (formerly the Rutgers Center for Innovative Print and Paper). In recognition of her commitment to the education of women artists, the Rutgers Libraries have established the Miriam Schapiro Archives for Women Artists.

Schapiro along with Judy Chicago created the first Feminist Art curriculum at the California Institute for the Arts in the early 1970s.

Alessandra Comini and her partner, the late Eleanor Tufts sit in front of the double portrait by Kyra, a Feminist artist living in Florida, who, herself, has been an active participant in the American Women's Movement in Art.

Comini is a distinguished professor emerita at Southern Methodist University. Professor Comini has published seven books, of which one, *Egon Schiele's Portraits* (1974, reissued in paperback, 1990), was nominated for the National Book Award and received the College Art Association's Charles Rufus Morey Book Award. Her other books are: *Schiele in Prison* (1973), *Gustav Klimt* (1975, with French, German, and Dutch editions; reissued 2001), *Egon Schiele* (1976, with Italian, French, German, and Dutch editions; reissued 2001), *The Fantastic Art of Vienna* (1978), *The Changing Image of Beethoven: A Study in Mythmaking* (1987), and *Egon Schiele Nudes* (1994).

Her new book, *Passionate Pursuit* reveals her passion for her work as a scholar and teacher. An unconventional art historian, Comini draws on her lifelong daily journals beginning with her own colorful background as a refugee from Franco's Spain, then Mussolini's Italy.

Eleanor Tufts was also a professor in art history at the Meadows School of the Arts, Southern Methodist. Tufts was the author of one of the first histories of women artists, *Our Hidden Heritage: Five Centuries of Women Artists*. published in 1974. She was the author of four other books including *Luis Melendez, 18th-Century Master of the Spanish Still Life* published in 1985 to accompany a Melendez exhibition which she organized at the National Academy of Design in New York City.

An American artist of Hispanic heritage (Argentina), Kyra Belan received her B. F. A. at Arizona State University and her M. F. A. at Florida State University, both degrees in Visual Arts. Her Ed. D., from Florida International University, is in Community College Education and Art History. Currently, Dr. Belan is professor of art and art history at Broward Community College, Pembroke Pines, Florida.

Kyra, as she is usually known in the circle of women artists, has been active in the Feminist Art Movement for decades. She is interested in celebrating women's bodies and women's sexuality.

The artist has had over 40 solo exhibitions and over 75 group exhibitions across the country and abroad, including Museum of Art, Ft. Lauderdale, FL; Boca Raton Museum of Art, FL; Kassell Museum, Germany; Lowe Museum of Art, Coral Gables, FL; and The Florida Museum of Hispanic and Latin American Art, among others.

Dr. Belan has co-authored a book about Dorothy Gillespie, published by Radford University Press, and is the author of a book titled *Earth, Spirit, Gender: Visual Language for the New Reality*, Forbes, 1996.

Kyra Belan has received numerous awards and grants, including an Artist Fellowship from Florida Arts Council, Barbara Deming Memorial Fund Grant and Outstanding Artist of the Southeast.

Comini and the artist, Kyra, in conversation at one of the Women's Caucus for Art (WCA) conferences. Notice the cowboy hat which is Comini's signature. The WCA and College Art Association conferences over the last 35 years have provided the opportunity for interaction among women artists, art historians, and other visual arts professionals. This interaction has been of great importance in generating ideas and projects in the Feminist Art Movement.

The Women's Caucus for Art was one of the first organizations established by women artists and art historians in the early 1970s. The WCA led the way in establishing the statistical base that proved discrimination against women in the art world. Studies showed that while 50% of the doctorates in art history were awarded to women, there were very few women on art history faculties--a shocking 10% or less--and at the bottom of the hierarchy. Studio faculties fared even more poorly, with only 3% of the faculty drawn from the ranks of women artists. And 70% of the undergraduates in studio classes were women! These studies inspired discrimination suits which were won by women and resulted in changes in hiring practice. Furthermore, the number of artists and art historians of color, whether male or female was miniscule. The lack of representation in the field of people of color can be seen in these photographs where there are very few. Today the situation, while not perfect, has greatly improved for both women and visual arts professionals of color. The Feminist Art Project reflects this change in that it is fully multi-cultural.

Today, the WCA has chapters across the United States and is an active participant in The Feminist Art Project, mounting exhibitions and programs that focus on the contributions of women artists. The records of the national organization are in the Miriam Schapiro Archives for Women Artists at Rutgers.

Dr. Comini is on the left. In the center is Whitney Chadwick, the author of several books on women artists including the very popular, *Women, Art, and Society*, used as a text book in courses on women artists at many universities today. Chadwick also wrote a crucial book documenting women artists involved with the Surrealist Movement.

On the right is Josephine Withers, professor emerita, University of Maryland. Withers was one of the founding members of the Women's Caucus for Art and participated in the founding of the Washington DC chapter of the WCA as well.

She specializes in the study of twentieth-century art. Her book *Julio Gonzalez: Sculpture in Iron* is a major monograph on the Catalan sculptor. Professor Withers is a leading figure in feminist scholarship, especially as it is applied to contemporary women's art. Her articles in that field have been included in many journals. Among other subjects, she has written on Judy Chicago's *Dinner Party*.

Her exhibition, *Women Artists in Washington Collections,* like Nochlin's and Sutherland's exhibition, *Women Artists 1550 - 1950*, required dusty research In the basements of Washington museums. The exhibition resulted in the way in which the collections in these museums were subsequently hung, giving more space to the work of women artists.

Withers was one of the organizers of the National Conference of Women in the Visual Arts, held in Washington, DC.

Alessandra Comini is pictured here with Gloria Steinem.

The Feminist Art Movement is important to leadership in the women's rights movement. Artists, art historians, and critics ultimately play a large role in shaping how a culture views women. By changing the representation of women, artists help to change the paradigm of women in the society. Artists who show the female nude from women's perspective rather than as the object of male desire (the traditional depiction of women's bodies since the Renaissance) open the eyes of the public to a new view of female sexuality and gender.

The Women's Caucus for Art and women art professionals have participated in all the global conferences on women sponsored by the United Nations over the last few decades.

Eleanor Tufts is pictured here on the right with Pamela Askew, distinguished professor emerita, Vassar College, in 1988 at the College Art Association. Dr. Askew received the CAA Award for exceptional work in Art History. Tufts was chair of the committee.

The award to Askew is particularly significant in that it represents the change in attitude towards women art historians and recognition of their achievement in the field. Askew was an important Renaissance and Baroque scholar, particularly on Seventeenth Century painting with special emphasis on Caravaggio, Lorrain, and Rembrandt. She published many books and articles in key art historical journals. In addition, she was involved in wide ranging intellectual circles beyond Art History.

Here is Ann Sutherland Harris with her son, a small child during the period she was working on *Women Artists: 1550 - 1950*. Harris was teaching in New York, first at Columbia University and then at Hunter. She received substantial grant support from the Ford Foundation to work on the exhibition and catalogue.

Subsequently Harris moved to the University of Pittsburgh where she still teaches. In addition to her work on women artists, her specialty is seventeenth century European art.

Like many of the women active in the Feminist Art Movement, Ann Sutherland Harris has many talents, including playing the harp.

Dr. Harris was involved in the Feminist Art Movement even before co-curating the exhibition, *Women Artists: 1550 - 1950,* with Linda Nochlin. Harris was the founder of the Women's Caucus for Art in 1972. She asked the College Art Association (CAA), which was holding its annual conference in Detroit that year, for a small room in which to hold a meeting of CAA women members. She expected a few women to join her. The meeting was only announced with flyers during the conference rather than in advance. What happened is that the room filled to overflowing and the Women's Caucus for Art was created on the spot. Harris was elected the first president by acclamation.

In the mid '70s, the WCA was asked by the CAA to separate and become an organization on its own. By the late '70s the WCA numbered over 1,500 members.

Comini is here on the left with the artist Audrey Flack on the right. Flack was active in the Feminist Art Movement from the start.

She is one of the best known artists in the Photo Realist Movement of the early 1970s. Her elegant, photographic-like paintings have a complex intellectual content ranging from the Holocaust to vanity. Flack has also imbued women with heroic stature in a number of public commissions. In 1991 the city of Rock Hill, South Carolina invited her to do the sculptures for the gateway to the city. Flack created *Civitas: Four Visions: Gateway to the City of Rock Hill*, four bronze figures, rising to a height of 20 feet each. In 1992, the city of Queens, New York selected Flack as the winner of the international competition to build a monument to Catherine of Braganza, a Portuguese princess who became Queen of England and who is the namesake of the Borough of Queens, within the Queens West Development Project on the East River opposite the United Nations. This nine story sculpture will be second in size only to the Statue of Liberty.

On the right in this photograph is Thalia Gouma Peterson. Next to her is Muriel Magenta. Gouma Peterson died in in 2000. She was a professor of art history and the museum director at the College of Wooster in Wooster, Ohio. She began and remained, an expert on Byzantine art, but she became a significant contributor to the documentation of contemporary women artists. She curated exhibitions and wrote about Miriam Schapiro, Elizabeth Catlett, Audrey Flack, Faith Ringgold, Joyce Kozloff, and Michelle Stuart.

Gouma Peterson was the primary author of Abrams' *Breaking the Rules: Audrey Flack: A Retrospective 1950-1990;* general editor of *Miriam Schapiro, A Retrospective, 1953-1980,* a catalogue for a traveling exhibition she organized at the College of Wooster in 1980; *Miriam Schapiro: Shaping the Fragments of Art and Life* (1999); and *Hung Liu: A Survey 1988-1998* (paper, 1997).

With Patricia Matthews, she wrote a long essay for the *Art Bulletin* in the early '80s, that laid out the differences between 1970s Feminist Art ideas and those of the early 1980s. The earlier period was described as essentialist, focusing as it did on women as constructed by society whereas in the 1980s the focus was on deconstructing that image.

Muriel Magenta, a professor at Arizona State University where she heads an experimental media center, was a president of the Women's Caucus for Art in the mid 1980s. Magenta works in video, computer art, web technology, installation, multimedia performance, and sculpture. Magenta's video works have been screened internationally and throughout the U.S. She organized video screenings of works by women artists at three international women's conferences--Copenhagen, Nairobi, and Beijing.

Ofelia Garcia (on the left) has made an significant imprint on the education of artists in the United States. Starting out as a printmaker and professor at Boston College, she became the director of The Print Center, Philadelphia. Already involved in the Feminist Art Movement, she became national president of the Women's Caucus for Art in the early 1980s. Garcia moved to the presidency of the Atlanta College of Art. Returning to Philadelphia, she became the president of Rosemont College. She now teaches at William Paterson University, New Jersey, where she has just stepped down as dean of the College of Fine Arts and Communication.

Lee Anne Miller has been another influential educator. She was teaching at Wayne State University in Detroit when she first became involved In the Feminist Art Movement. Miller was national president of the WCA in the late 1970s. It was during her presidency that four women artists, Isabel Bishop, Selma Burke, Alice Neel, Louise Nevelson, and Georgia O'Keeffe were honored at the White House. Miller went on to become dean of The Cooper Union School of Art.

Barbara Zucker, on the right, was co-founder of A.I.R. Gallery, New York, the first cooperative women artists' gallery in the early 1970s and one of the members of the Heresies Collective which published a major journal of the Feminist Art Movement. The papers of the Heresies Collective reside at Rutgers in the MIrIam Schapiro Archives for Women Artists.

She currently teaches at the University of Vermont and has taught at Skowhegan, Princeton, and Yale. Zucker's work as an artist centers around aspects of the female body and experience. A recent exhibition consisted of drawings based on the wrinkles of the face as one gets older. Zucker says the drawings are in a sense, a self portrait. Another exhibition focused on all the routines women have for grooming from eyebrow tweezing to leg shaving.

The late Lila Katzen was a sculptor who worked in large scale metal. Her work was very well known during her lifetime, but has slipped in recognition since her death, an example of the way in which women artists disappear from the historical record.

Katzen was a feminist from the beginning. Active in teaching as well as in organizations like the College Art Association and the Women's Caucus for Art, she defied gender stereotypes with her monumental sculptures.

Starting from the left, Eleanor Tufts, Ann Sutherland Harris, and Alessandra Comini stand in front of the entrance to Judy Chicago's *Dinner Party* in its original incarnation in the 1970s.

The *Dinner Party* has now taken on iconic status. It is to be re-installed at the Brooklyn Museum as the centerpiece of the new Ellizabeth A. Sackler Center for Feminist Art, which is under the direction of curator Maura Reilly. The opening of the Sackler Center will take place in March 2007. Accompanying the Dinner Party will be an exhibition, *Global Feminisms*, curated by Reilly and Linda Nochlin that will display the art of women artists born after 1960. This gala event is one of the major events in The Feminist Art Project.

The *Dinner Party* consists of some 39 place settings around a triangle shaped table. It elevates female achievement in Western history to the heroic scale traditionally reserved for men. The *Dinner Party* is a massive ceremonial banquet in art, laid on a triangular shaped table measuring forty-eight feet on each side. Combining the glory of sacramental tradition with the intimate detail of a carefully orchestrated social gathering, Chicago represents 39 guests of honor by individually symbolic, larger-than-life-size china-painted porcelain plates rising from intricate textiles draped completely over the tabletop. Each plate features an image based on the butterfly, symbolic of a vaginal central core. The runners name the 39 women and bear images drawn from each one's story. Chicago worked with many artists on the creation of the elements that form the place settings.

At the table from left to right are the artist and founder of Tamarind Lithography Workshop, June Wayne; Allison Hilton, art historian at Georgetown University, Ruth Weisberg, artist, dean of the School of Fine Arts, University of Southern California; and Alessandra Comini.

June Wayne is one of the founders of the Feminist Art Movement in Los Angeles. In the early 1970s, as "Joan of Art," she ran a series of workshops to help women artists learn the business of art. By then she had turned Tamarind over to the University of New Mexico after running the workshop for a decade, funded by the Ford Foundation. Wayne revived the art of lithography in the United States by training lithographers and developing techniques for collaboration between artists and printers. Wayne is now a Distinguished Visiting Research Professor at the Brodsky Center for Print and Paper at Rutgers and has given a collection of her work and the work of other artists to the Mason Gross School of the Arts which has established the June Wayne Archive and Study Center.

Ruth Weisberg is well known for her extraordinary narrative paintings about women and Judaism. She has participated in the Feminist Art Movement since the early 1970s. In 1977 she formed a chapter of the Women's Caucus for Art in Los Angeles and worked with Judith K. Brodsky to mount the first full blown conference held by the Women's Caucus for Art. In the 1980s, Weisberg was elected to the board of the College Art Association and served as president of the CAA. She was also a long time officer of the national Women's Caucus for Art.

Arlene Raven died unexpectedly in 2006 in the midst of her extraordinary career as an art historian and critic. She was the author of seven books on contemporary art and wrote criticism for *The Village Voice* and a variety of newspapers, art magazines, exhibition catalogues, and scholarly journals as diverse as *Ms.*, *October*, and *The New York Daily News* since 1969. Raven taught widely and at the time of her death was a faculty member at the Maryland Institute College of Art, where a memorial scholarship has been founded in her name.

She was central to the Feminist Art Movement, having been a founder of the Women's Caucus for Art, the Los Angeles Woman's Building, and *Chrysalis* magazine. In addition, she was an architect of the educational programs of the Feminist Studio Workshop, an independent school at the Woman's Building.

Raven's selected essays were published as *Crossing Over: Feminism and Art of Social Concern* in 1988 in UMI Research Press's American Art Critics series. She was an author and editor of *Feminist Art Criticism: An Anthology* (UMI, 1988; Harper/Collins, 1993), *New Feminist Art* (Harper/Collins, 1993), and *Art in the Public Interest* (UMI, 1989; Da Capo, 1994). She was an author of *Exposures: Women The Art* (NewSage, 1989). Her monographs are *Nancy Grossman* (Hillwood Art Museum, 1991) and *June Wayne: Tunnel of the Senses* (Neuberger Museum, 1997).

Raven won grants from the California Arts Commission, The Samuel H. Kress Foundation, and was the recipient of two National Endowment for the Arts art critics' fellowships. She was recognized by Hood College in 1997 with a Doctor of Humanities degree honoris causa. *Feminist Art Criticism* won the Susan Koppelman Award from the Women's Caucus of the Popular Culture Association/American Cultural Association for the best anthology of 1988.

Raven was a member of the national committee of The Feminist Art Project.

The founding of the Woman's Building in Los Angeles in 1973 was the culmination of several years of activity by women artists who were energized by the Feminist Art Movement. This activity included protests of major museums for their exclusion of women artists, the opening of gallery spaces dedicated to the work of women, the founding of the first feminist art education programs (in 1970, by Judy Chicago at Fresno State College and in 1971 by Judy Chicago and Miriam Schapiro at California Institute of the Arts), and the first large scale public feminist art installation, *Womanhouse*. In 1973. Artist Judy Chicago, graphic designer Sheila Levrant de Bretteville, and art historian Arlene Raven founded the first independent school for women artists, the Feminist Studio Workshop (FSW). The FSW focused not only on the development of artmaking skills (in visual arts, writing, performance art, video, graphic design and the printing arts), but also on the development of women's identity and sensibility, and the translation of these elements into their artwork. Central to the founders' vision was the idea that the arts should not be separated from other activities of the burgeoning women's community, and the three looked for a site for their school that could also be shared with other organizations and enterprises.

When the Woman's Building opened, hundreds of women came from across the United States (and from as far away as Canada, Mexico, Holland and Switzerland) to attend the FSW. The facility was also home to galleries, theater companies, Sisterhood Bookstore, Womantours Travel Agency, a coffeehouse, and the offices of the National Organization for Women. In 1981, the Woman's Building underwent major organizational change as a shift occurred in the cultural and economic climates of the United States. By that year, the organization's founders had all left to pursue other projects, and a "second generation" of FSW graduates would carry the organization through the next decade. That year the FSW closed, as the demand for alternative education diminished. Until its closing in 1991, the Woman's Building was an internationally recognized symbol of the vitality and substance of women's creative achievements.

Marilyn Stokstad is the Judith Harris Murphy distinguished professor of art history at the University of Kansas. Stockstad's 1995 art history survey textbook was the first art history survey to showcase women artists. The book has been adopted as the introductory art history textbook in hundreds of colleges and universities throughout the United States. In recognition of the fact that Stoskstad has helped to prevent the erasure of women artists from history, the National Women's Caucus for Art bestowed an Honor Award on her in 2002.

A strong supporter of women in leadership roles, Stokstad was the second woman president of the College Art Association, a national organization of artists and art historians, and was president of the International Center of Medieval Art.

The photograph shows Linda Nochlin receiving an award from the Women's Caucus for Art and showing her determination to keep women artists from erasure in the annals of art history.

On the left is Cindy Nemser, who was the editor in chief of the first glossy magazine devoted to women artists, *The Feminist Art Journal (FAJ)*, published from 1972 to 1977. She was founder of the magazine along with co-founders, Pat Mainardi and Irene Moss. The magazine gives a view of the Feminist Art Movement on the East Coast. The FAJ had articles on issues ignored by other art magazines of the time, issues of narrative art and autobiographical art and introduced the idea that women were also art patrons by publishing the first articles on figures like Marie de Medici and her collecting. Nemser's *ArtTalk*, interviews with 17 women artists, is a landmark book, providing first hand documentation of the emerging Feminist Art Movement. Nemser curated an important exhibition of women's self portraits held during Philadelphia Focuses on Women in the Visual Arts, a city-wide festival in 1974 conceived by the artist, Diane Burko with Nemser.

On the right is Norma Broude, professor at American University and one of the founding members of the Women's Caucus for Art. Along with Mary Garrard, her colleague, Broude edited *The Power of Feminist Art*, published in 1993 by Abrams. Now in paperback, it remains in print and is the primary published source of information and anaylsis about The Feminist Art Movement of the 1970s.

On the left is the late Eleanor Tufts, professor of art history at Southern Methodist University and on the right, Judy Chicago, artist and creator of the *Dinner Party*.

The relationship between artists and art historians is not always a close one but that is not true of the artists and scholars involved in The Feminist Art Movement in the United States. The flow of ideas back and forth resulted in revolutionary work on both sides.

Mary Garrard is on the left and Norma Broude on the right. These two scholars, so vital to the Feminist Art Movement in the United States and elsewhere, have authored a number of books that cement women artists and the ideas and aesthetics of the Feminist Art Movement into the historical record. In addition to their conceiving and editing *The Power of Feminist Art*, the definitive survey of concepts and history of the Feminist Art Movement of the 1970s, a series of volumes with essays by various art historians use feminist principles to revise art history.

Reclaiming Female Agency is the third in their influential series of anthologies. It follows *Feminism and Art History: Questioning the Litany* (1982) and *Expanding The Discourse: Feminism and Art History* (1992). The new volume identifies female agency as a central theme of recent feminist scholarship. It includes twenty-three essays on artists and issues from the Renaissance to the present.

Garrard and Broude also publish individually. Garrard is the author of the monograph on Artemisia Gentileschi published by Princeton University Press, and Broude writes on French painting of the 19th century. In all their books, they write from a feminist perspective.

Garrard was the second national president of the Women's Caucus for Art, as well as one of its founding members. She succeeded in establishing the WCA as an organization distinct from the College Art Association. Broude was also a founding member of the WCA and organized a system to monitor job placement for women art historians and artists during the 1970s. Both women were honored by the CAA Committee on Women in the Arts.

In this photograph, the late Eleanor Tufts on the left speaks with Elsa Honig Fine in the center and Cynthia Navaretta on the right. Fine and Navaretta are two of the publishing giants of the Feminist Art Movement.

Fine was the publisher and editor of the *Woman's Art Journal* which she founded in 1979 to eliminate the erasure of women artists and which she continued to direct until 2006 when she retired. Rutgers University is now the umbrella for the *Woman's Art Journal* with Joan Marter as editor-in-chief. It would be difficult to count the number of women artists who have been brought to light through the *Woman's Art Journal,* ranging from historical figures of earlier centuries to artists of today. It is an essential reference for any study of the history of women in the visual arts.

Navaretta founded and published the *Women Artists Newsletter.* Based in New York, Navaretta covered the country through her ceaseless efforts to communicate widely. It comprehensive listings of events and exhibitions pertaining to women artists including its articles on various artists made it essential reading in the art world. In addition, Navaretta has published a series of books devoted to artists from various regions, artists of color, and directories for artists' grants and other services under the imprint of MidMarch Press.

Alessandra Comini and Eleanor Tufts are sitting in Judy Chicago's studio with women artists who were working on aspects of the *Dinner Party*. Chicago designed the plates for the place setting and other artists participated in designing the place runners, cutlery, crystal, and other accoutrements of formal dining. The *Dinner Party* involved scholars as well as artists for the research that was necessary. The complete installation first opened in 1979 in the San Franciscso Museum of Modern Art.

Eleanor Tufts, professor of Art History, Southern Methodist University, also served a term as member of the College Art Association (CAA) board. Here she is with Ann Coffin Hanson, the first woman president of the College Art Association from 1972 - 1974 on the far left of the picture; Rose Weil, the director of the CAA until 1986 on the near right; and Minerva Navarette, the Business Manager of the CAA under Weil's tenure. Ann Hanson was also the first female professor at Yale where she had a distinguished career.

In those days, the 1970s and early 1980s, the CAA was a sleepy learned society until the Feminist Art Movement shook it awake. The office staff was very small with only some clerical help beyond Weil and Navarette. The situation changed in 1986 when Weil retired and Susan Ball became executive director. Ball and Paul Arnold, then president, undertook a strategic planning process which resulted in an organization that was much more responsive to its membership. Since over half the members are women professionals in the field, CAA has been a friendly environment for Feminist Art as can be seen in the annual conferences where many of the panels address Feminist Art history and Feminist Art.

The College Art Association is a founding partner of The Feminist Art Project. In February 2007, at the annual conference, this year in New York, there will be a full day of panels devoted to Feminist Art.

Women from the Feminist Art Movement participated in the national and international women's conferences held during lthe 1980s and 1990s. In this photograph from the conference in 1987, you can glimpse Bella Abzug in one of her trademark hats behind the microphone.

In 1980, the College Art Association Annual Conference was held in New Orleans. Many members of the Women's Caucus for Art decided to boycott the New Orleans conference because Louisiana had not signed the Equal Rights Amendment (ERA). They decided to hold an alternative conference in Washington DC. At the alternative conference, the artists and art historians would not do business as usual (meaning to talk about art). They would focus on the leaders of the Women's Movement in the United States and on the broader issues of political and social advancement for women. The leaders were honored at a special ceremony at which they were given works of art by feminist artists. Bella Abzug was one of the honorees at that event. She was given a print by Judith K. Brodsky. Gloria Steinem was honored with a print by Miriam Schapiro.

Shown here are Bella Abzug and Betty Friedan at the 1987 national conference on the status of women.

Shown here are longtime colleagues and friends, Ruth Weisberg, artist and dean of the Roski School of Fine Arts at University of Southern California on the left, and June Wayne, artist and founder of Tamarind Lithography Workshop, on the right.

The photograph of Stella Kramrisch, for many years curator of Indian art at the Philadelphia Museum of Art shows her receiving a Life Time Achievement Award from the Women's Caucus for Art in 1983. The Life Time Achievement Awards give recognition to pioneering art historians as well as artists.

Kramrisch was a groundbreaking interpreter of Indian art and its religious contexts. During her entire career as a creative scholar, teacher, museum curator and editor, she was a dominant force in shaping European, American, and Asian notions of Indian culture. From 1921-50 she taught at the University of Calcutta. During those years she edited the *Journal of the Indian Society of Oriental Art* and published numerous works including her magnum opus, *The Hindu Temple* (1946). She traveled to the U.S. as early as 1922, but after the assassination of her husband in Pakistan (1950), she moved permanently to the United States where she taught at the Institute of Fine Art, New York University, the University of Pennsylvania and was a curator at the Philadelphia Museum of Art.

The relationship between the Feminist Art Movement and the larger women's rights movement is a strong one. This photograph captures The Honorable Sissy Farenthold (on the left) at a women's conference in which feminist artists and art historians participated. Farenthold served two terms in the Texas House, representing Nueces and Kleberg counties (near and including Corpus Christi), from 1968 to 1972, and went on to run for the Texas Governor's office in 1972, and to receive over 400 votes for nomination as Vice President at the Democratic National Convention that same year. During her career in Texas state politics, she was an early critic of environmental regulation in the state, challenging various conflicts of interest, barriers to public participation, redlining of industrial areas, use of discretionary loopholes, and so on.